BASIC ART TECHNIQUES

BASIC ART TECHNIQUES

CLAUDIA HINDU

President & Founder of Claudia's Art Therapy

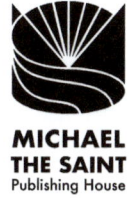

MICHAEL THE SAINT
Publishing House

This book is dedicated to God who inspires me & to those who have inspired me throughout my life.

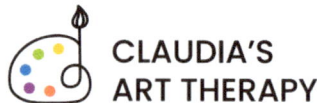

CLAUDIA'S ART THERAPY

Author: Claudia Hindu

Copyright © 2021 by Claudia Hindu

Cover design by Bethany Fuchigami-Campbell
Book interior design by Bethany Fuchigami-Campbell

All rights reserved. No part of this book may be reproduced or used in any manner without prior written permission of the copyright owner.

The scanning, uploading, electronic, mechanical, photocopying, recording or otherwise stored in a retrieval system or transmitted in any form or by any means sharing of any part of this book without the permission of the publisher is unlawful piracy and theft of the author's intellectual property. If you would like to use material from the book, prior written permission must be obtained by contacting the author. Thank you for your support of the author's rights.

Michael the Saint Publishing House
The publisher is not responsible for websites (or their content) that are not owned by the publisher.

Claudia's Art Therapy provides a wide range of topics for speaking events. To find out more, go to www.ClaudiasArtTherapy.com or call (323) 602-8982.

First Edition: June 2021
Bell, CA

Library of Congress Control Number 2021909218

IBSN: 978-1-7356868-3-7 (Hardcover), 978-1-7356868-9-9 (Paperback), 978-1-7356868-1-3 (E-book)

Printed in the United States of America

TABLE OF CONTENTS

7   *Claudia's Art Material Recommendations*

8   *Alternative Ways to Hold Your Pencil*

9   *Drawing a Square*

10   *Minimum Shading*

11   *Maximum Shading*

12   *Drawing a Fruit Bowl*

14   *Watercolor*

16   *Drawing a Vase & Flowers*

18   *Drawing Figures*

20   *Drawing a Head & Face*

22   *Perspectives*

24   *Drawing Buildings*

26   *Drawing a Wall or Landscape*

28   *Animals & Textures*

CLAUDIA'S ART MATERIAL RECOMMENDATIONS

General tips:
- *You don't need overly priced materials to make good art. Affordable art materials will do the job.*
- *When you have a choice, non-toxic materials are the way to go.*

PAPER

When starting out, use thick white paper or low cost watercolor paper.

PENCILS

When drawing lightly, try using a mechanical pencil that has it's lead exposed at least 1/4 inch. This way it doesn't carve into the paper & easily erases. You can use the guide below when choosing pencils.

WATERCOLORS

Most watercolors will do. When starting out, a palette is preferable to paint tubes.

Use a small cup of water & have napkins on hand in case there is a spill. Napkins are also helpful for checking color or removing excess water.

Watercolor is a fundamental art skill. Once you master it, other media becomes easier to learn.

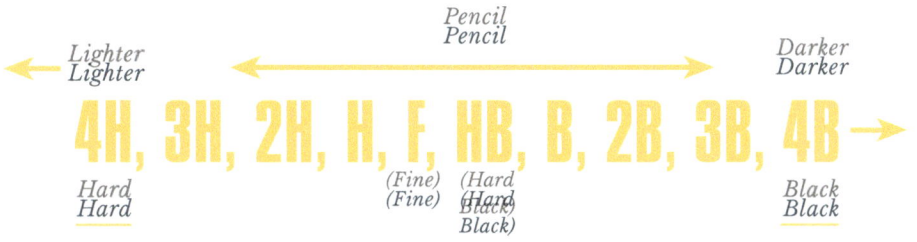

ALTERNATIVE WAYS TO HOLD YOUR PENCIL

Wrist should be relaxed.

Hold the pencil gently & low...

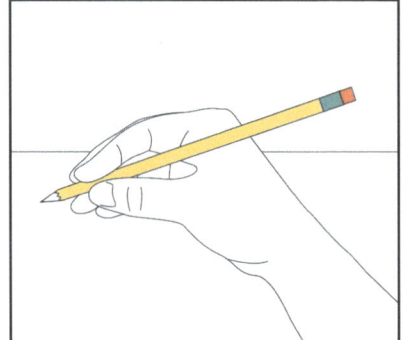

or

Center of your palm...

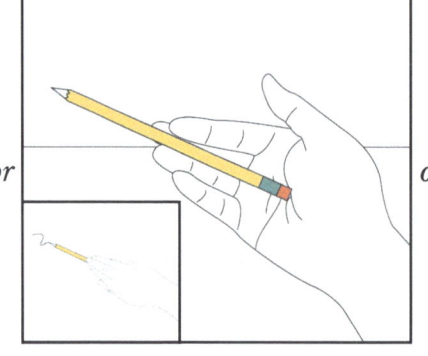

or

Between your thumb & pointer finger...

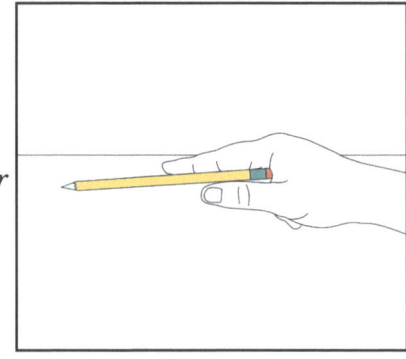

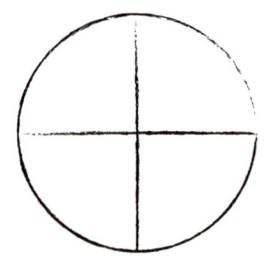

Practice by drawing 3 circles & squares using these techniques.

Add a "plus sign" to the center of your shape to check that all 4 sides match.

For a tutorial on "Alternative Ways to Hold Your Pencil", go to:
Claudia's Art Therapy YouTube Channel

DRAWING A SQUARE

Hold pencil gently & low so that your wrist is relaxed.

Always draw under your nose when drawing straight lines.

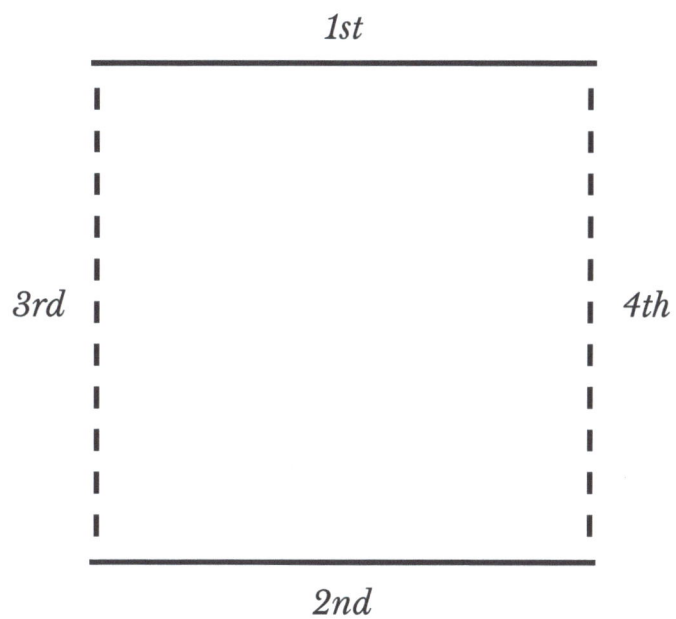

DRAWING A 3D SQUARE

1.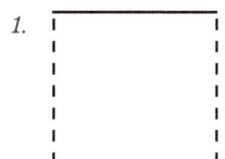
2.
3.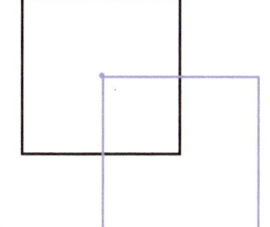
4.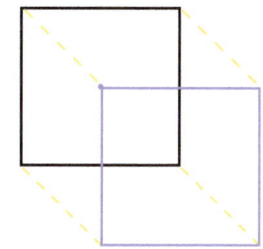

For a tutorial on "Drawing a Square", go to:
Claudia's Art Therapy YouTube Channel

MINIMUM SHADING

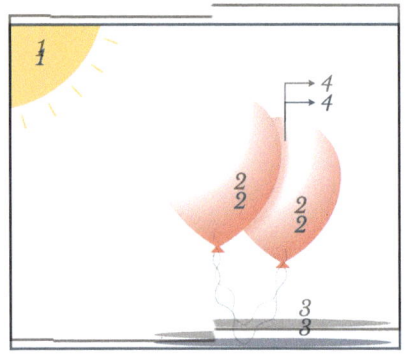 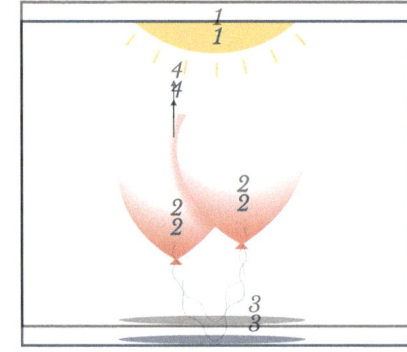 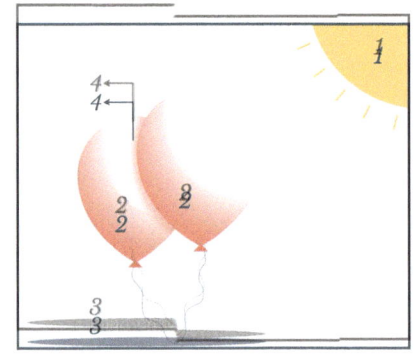

1: Choose source of light.
2: Shade opposite of object(s).
3: Shade outer parts of object(s).
4: Shade anything that overlaps.

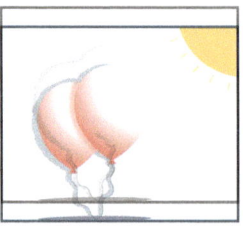

Sometimes there is a shadow behind the object. That tells us that there is something behind the object like a wall or another object.

For a tutorial on "Minimum Shading", go to:
Claudia's Art Therapy YouTube Channel

MAXIMUM SHADING

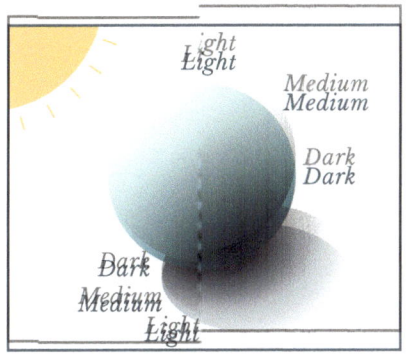 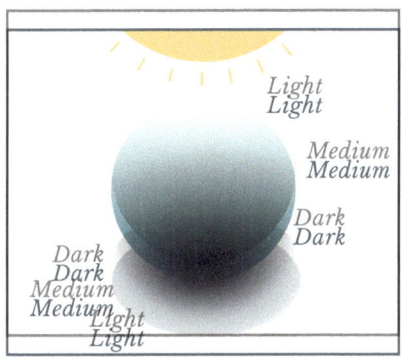 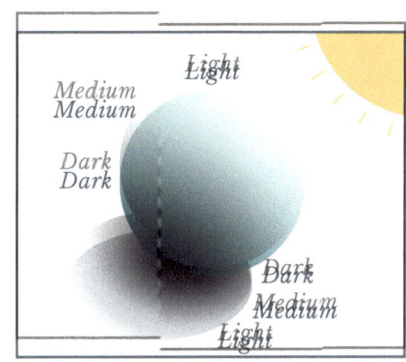

If you master shading, your drawings will look more realistic.
You can blend your shadows with your finger.

For a tutorial on "Maximum Shading", go to:
Claudia's Art Therapy YouTube Channel

DRAWING A FRUIT BOWL

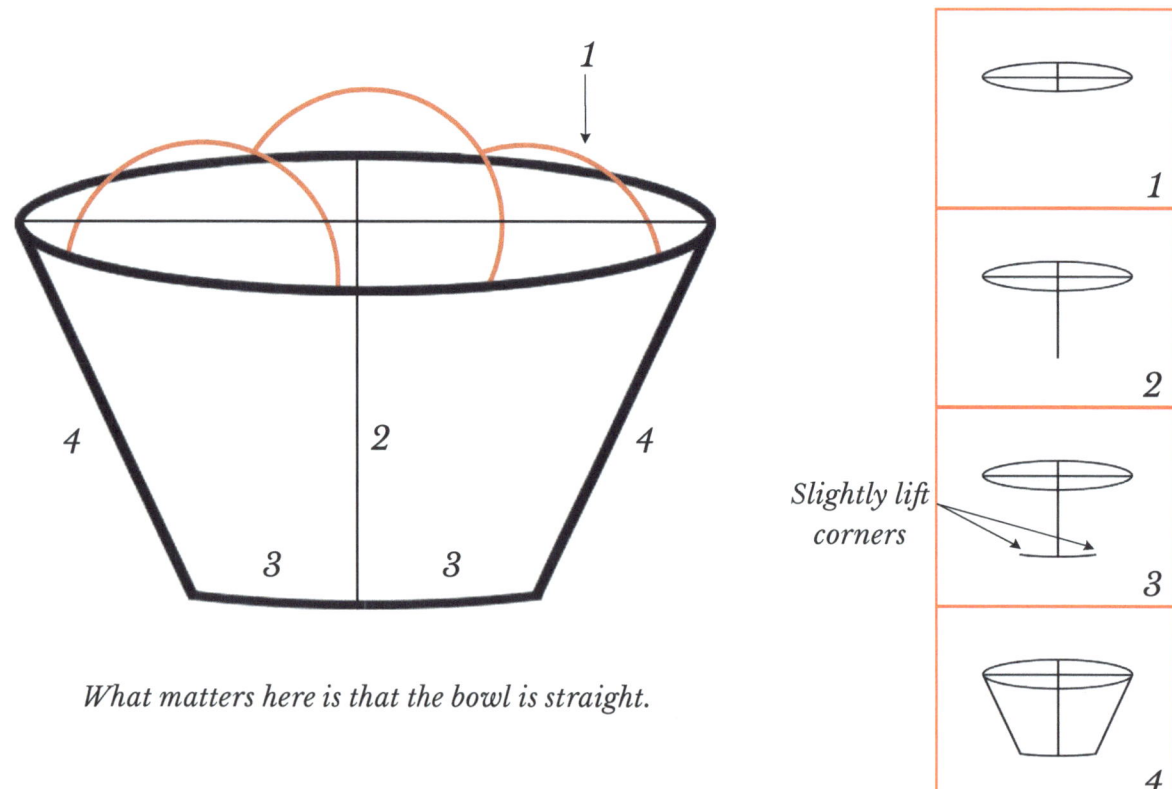

What matters here is that the bowl is straight.

Slightly lift corners

For a tutorial on "Drawing a Fruit Bowl", go to:
Claudia's Art Therapy YouTube Channel

NOW IT'S YOUR TURN!

Practice drawing a fruit bowl using the space below.

Try adding fruits like apples, oranges, & grapes, then add shadows to your drawing.

WATERCOLOR

MATERIALS NEEDED

Thick white paper or low cost watercolor paper

Watercolor paints, any kind will work

Thin, round paintbrush

Small container of water

Paper or cloth napkin

STEPS

1. 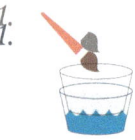 *dip your brush in* **WATER**

2. 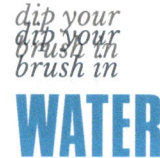 *choose your* **COLOR**

3. 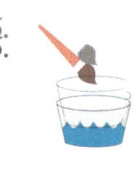 *Dab on* **NAPKIN**

4. 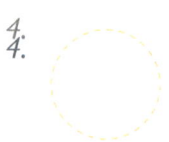 **OUTLINE**

5. 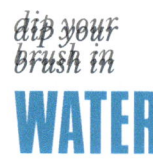 *dip your brush in* **WATER**

6. 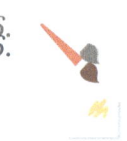 *Dab on* **NAPKIN**

7. 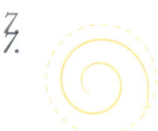 **PULL** *color from outline*

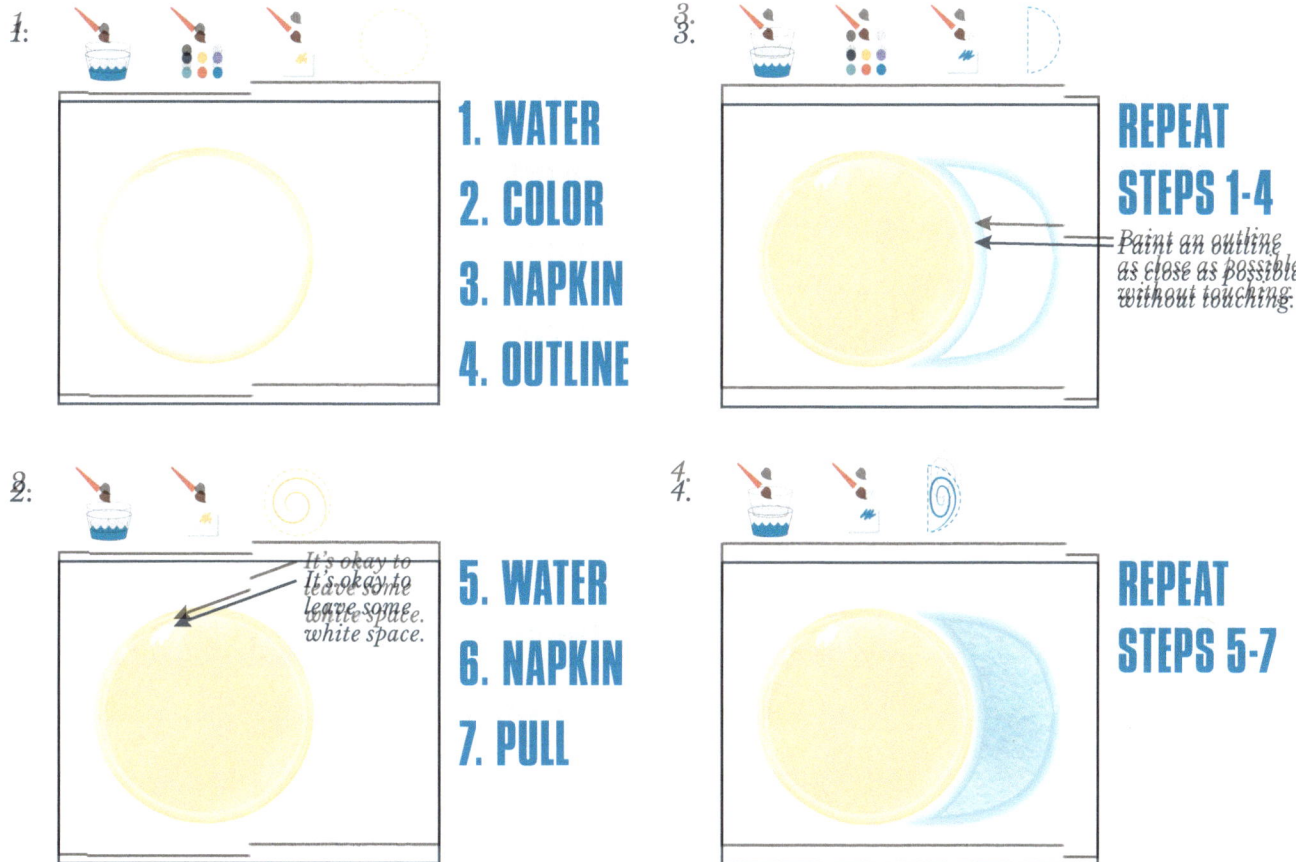

For a tutorial on "Watercolor", go to:
Claudia's Art Therapy YouTube Channel

DRAWING A VASE & FLOWERS

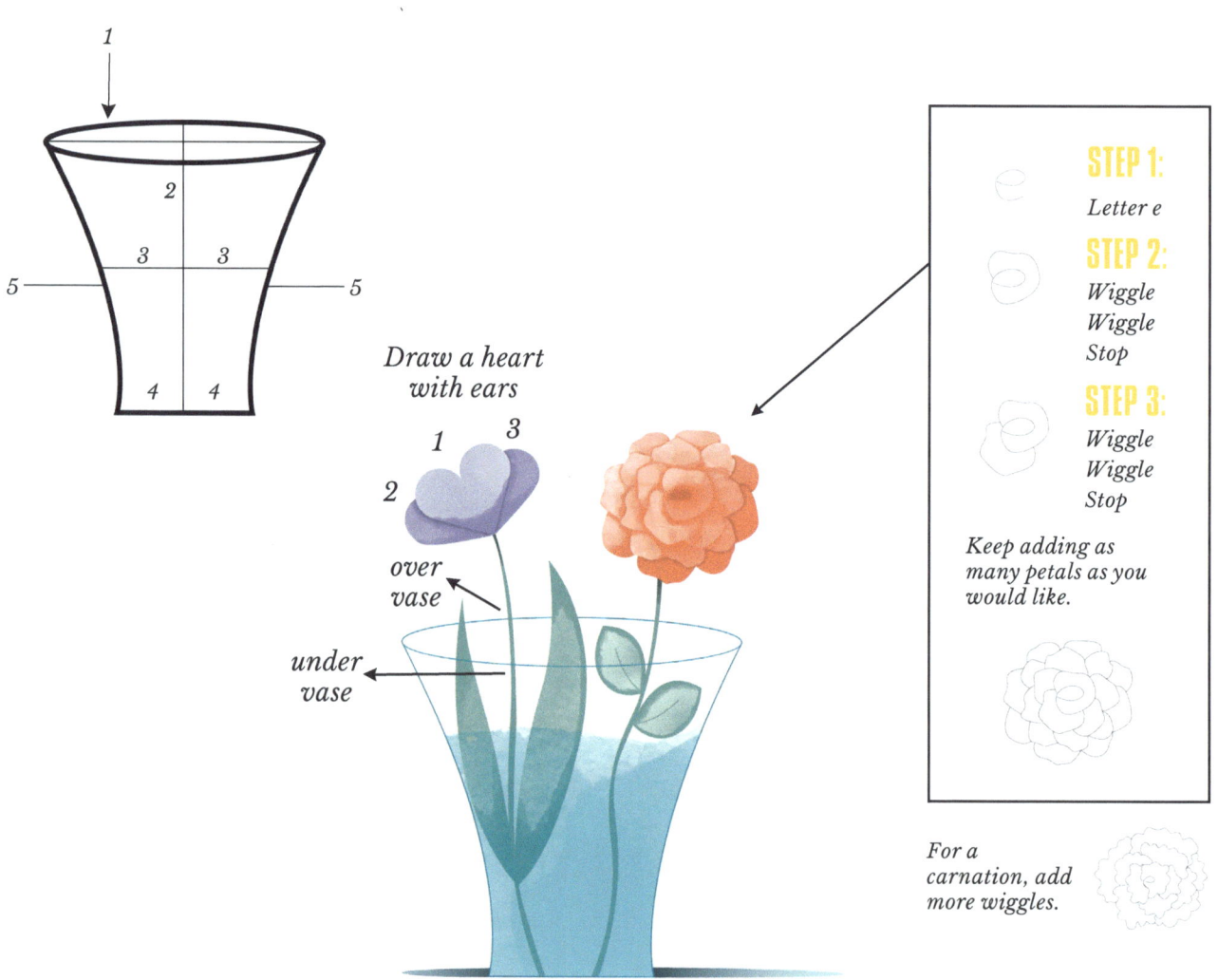

For a tutorial on "Drawing a Vase & Flowers", go to:
Claudia's Art Therapy YouTube Channel

NOW IT'S YOUR TURN!

Try drawing a vase & flowers using the space below.
Practice using your shading too.

DRAWING FIGURES

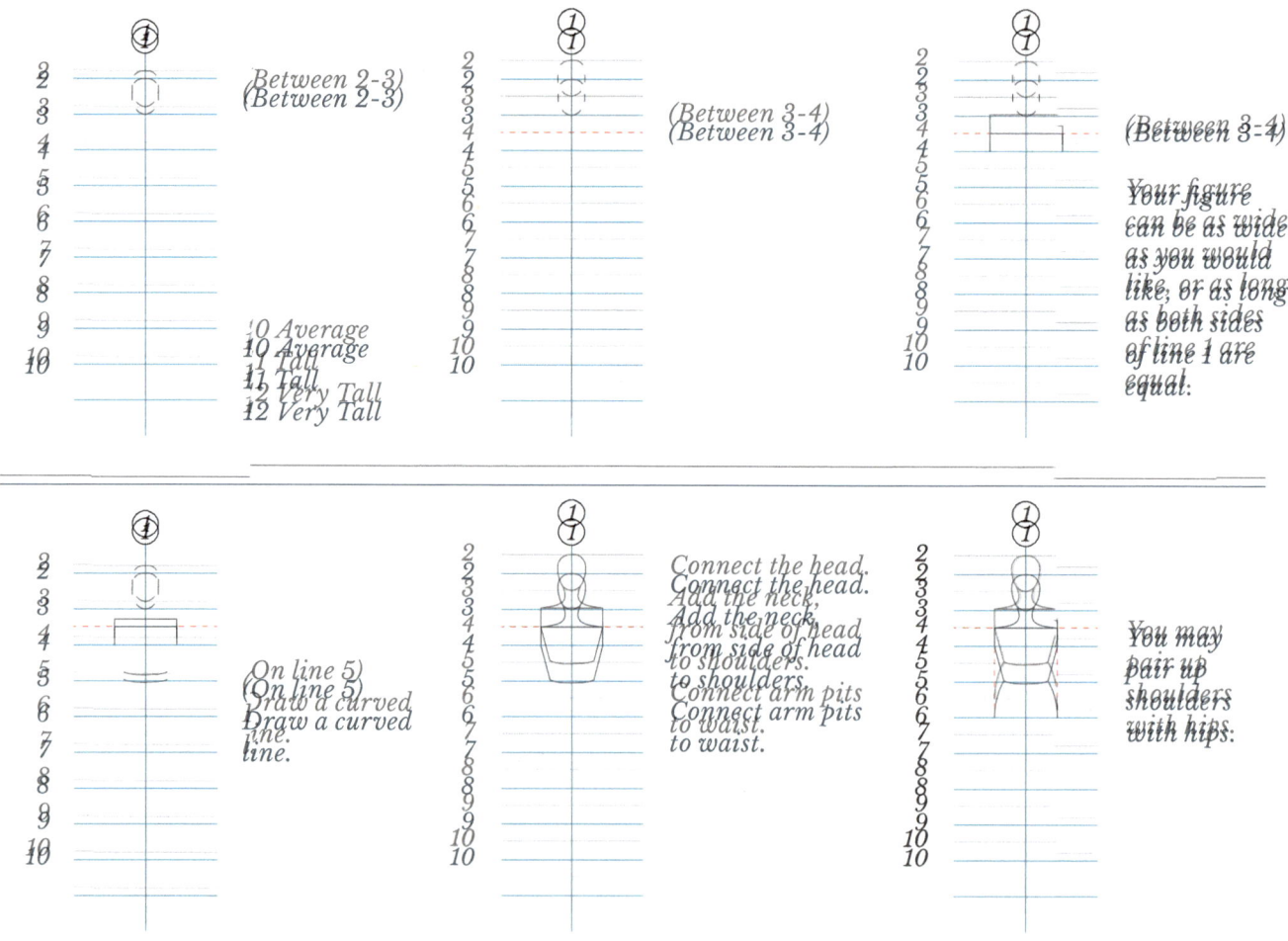

For a tutorial on "Drawing Figures", go to:
Claudia's Art Therapy YouTube Channel

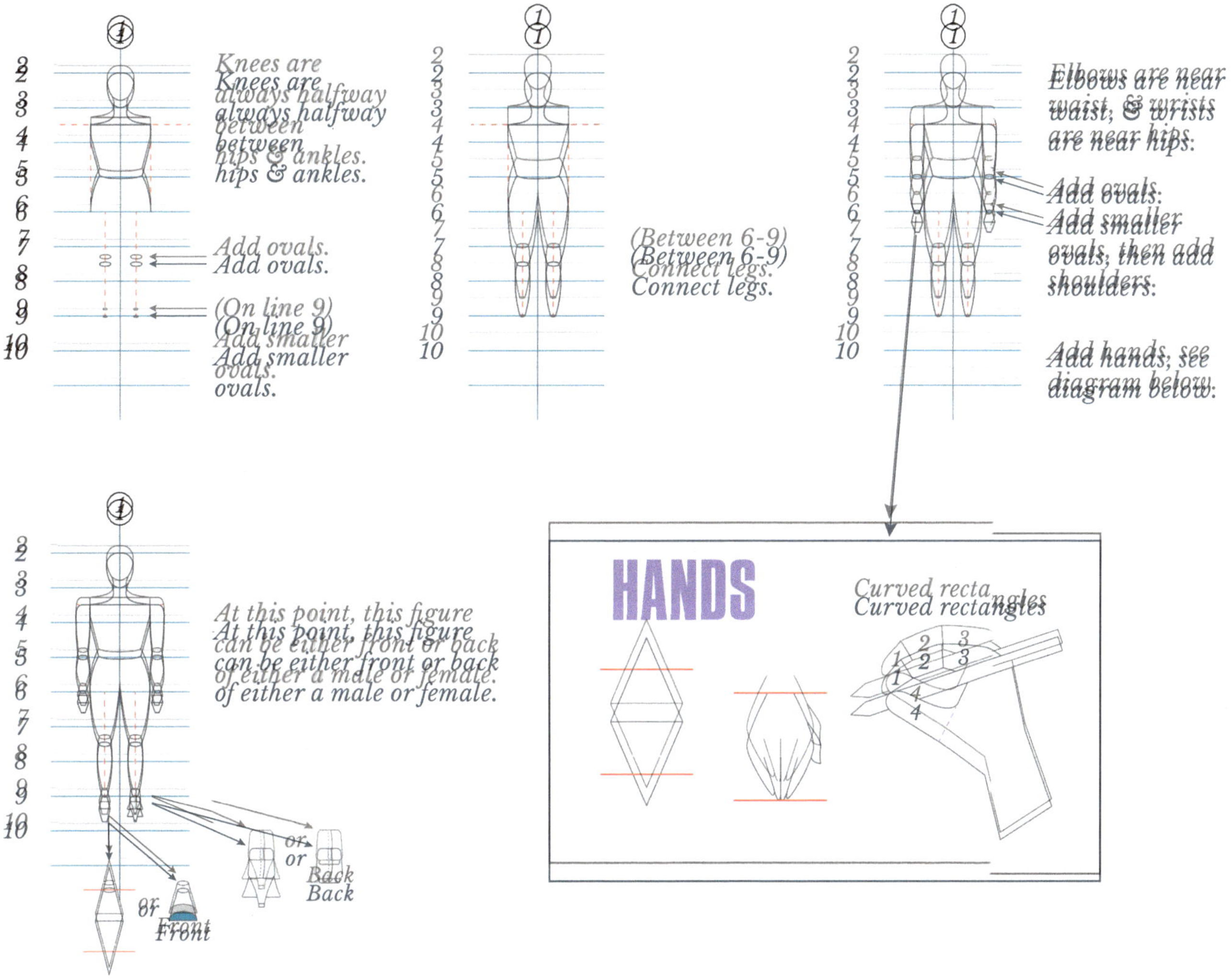

Knees are always halfway between hips & ankles.

Add ovals.

(On line 9) Add smaller ovals.

(Between 6-9) Connect legs.

Elbows are near waist, & wrists are near hips.

Add ovals.

Add smaller ovals, then add shoulders.

Add hands, see diagram below.

At this point, this figure can be either front or back of either a male or female.

or Front or Back

HANDS

Curved rectangles

DRAWING A HEAD & FACE

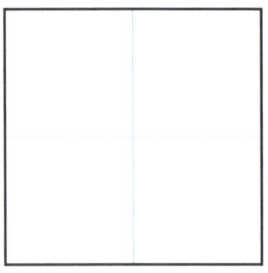
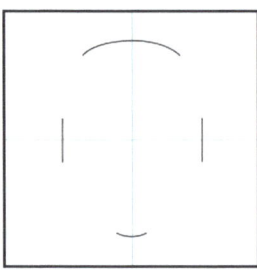
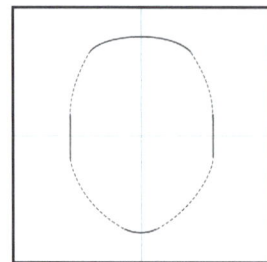
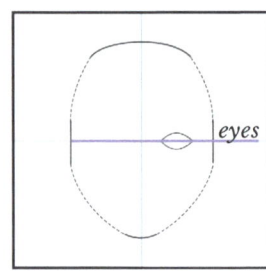

eyes — Eyes are placed in the center of head.

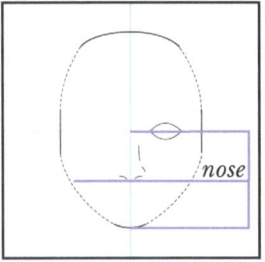
nose

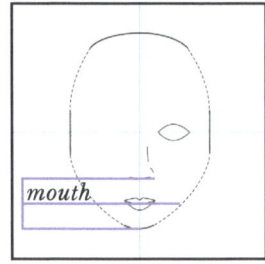
mouth

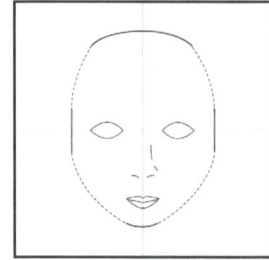

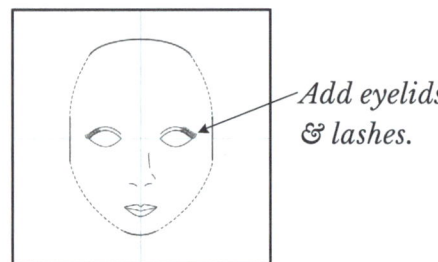
Add eyelids & lashes.

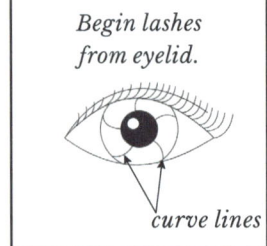
Begin lashes from eyelid.
curve lines

Add eyebrows & ears (no rule, just near eyes).

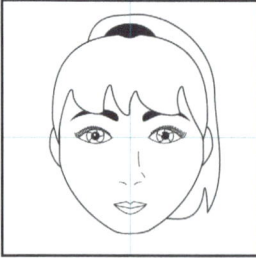

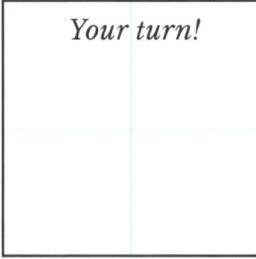
Your turn!

Study various faces & use this guide to help you.

For a tutorial on "Drawing a Head & Face", go to:
Claudia's Art Therapy YouTube Channel

NOW IT'S YOUR TURN!

Try drawing a body & face using the larger space below.
Practice your shading too!

PERSPECTIVES

1 POINT PERSPECTIVE

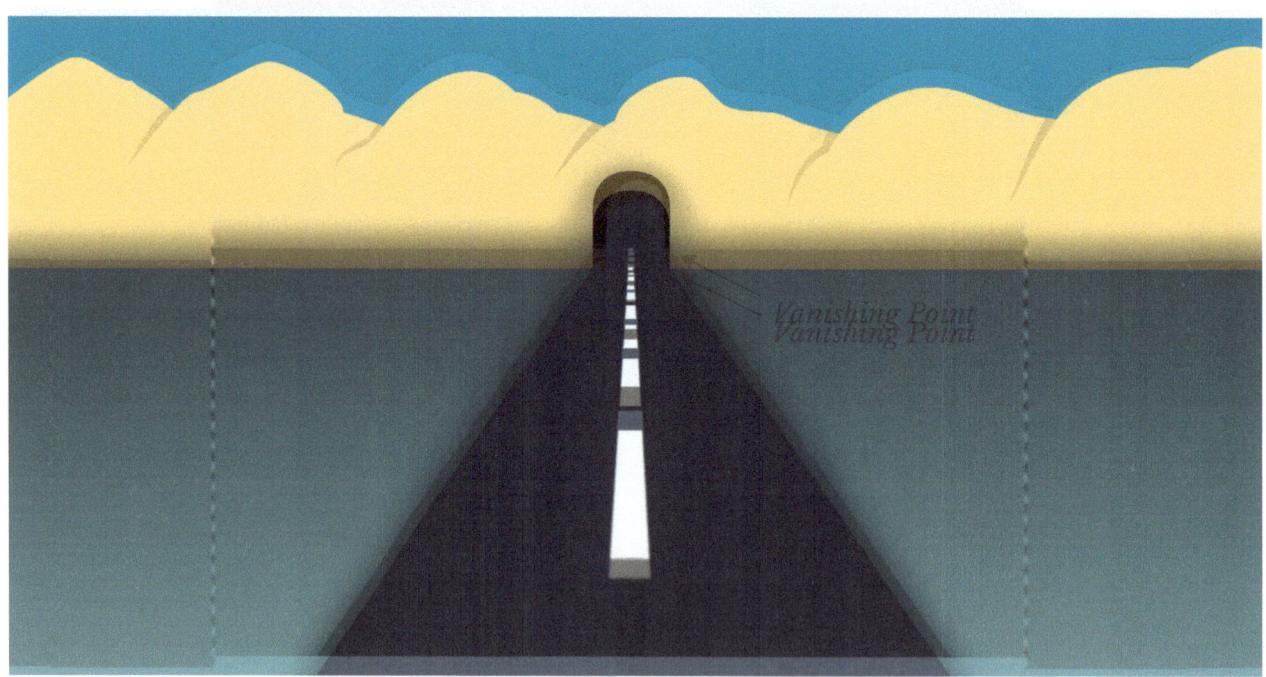

For a tutorial on "Perspectives", go to:
Claudia's Art Therapy YouTube Channel

2 POINT PERSPECTIVE

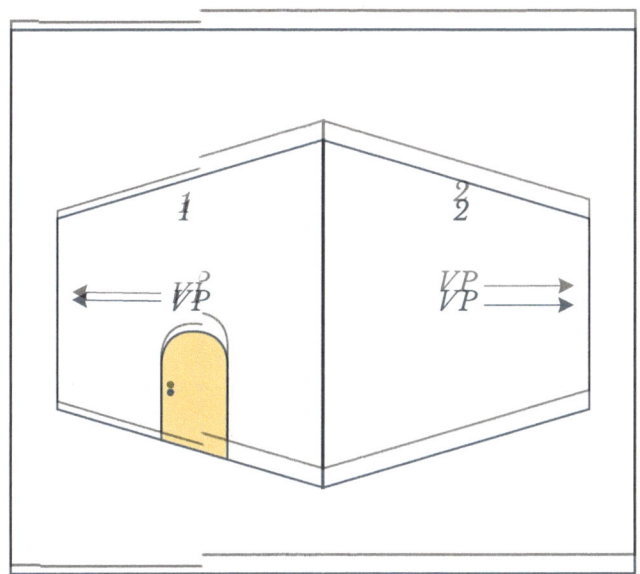

Vanishing Point = VP

3 POINT PERSPECTIVE

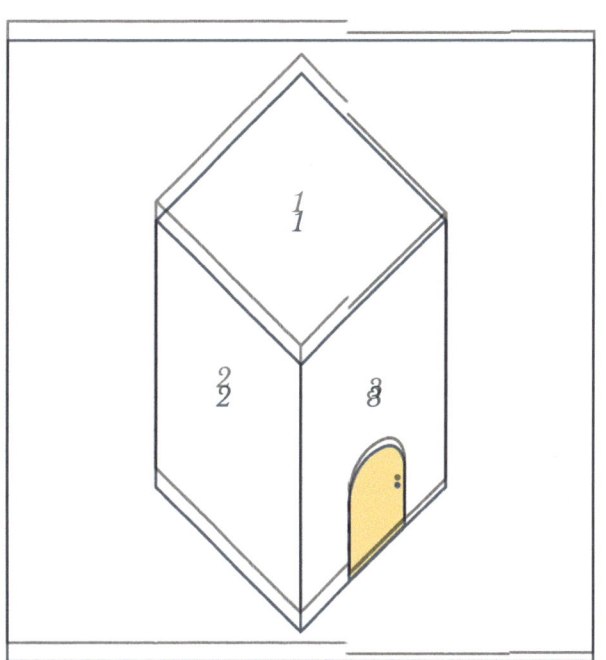

DRAWING BUILDINGS

STEPS

1. Find the hidden shapes.
2. Trace them.
3. Draw it on another paper.
4. Start with the largest shape first (in this case it's a rectangle).

Tip:
Draw mass before detail.

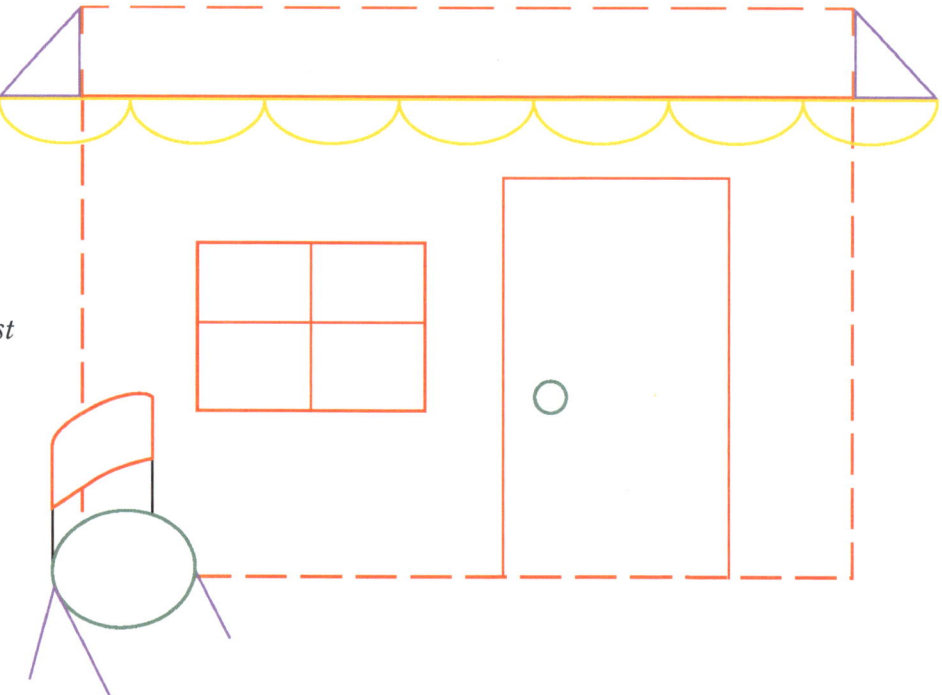

For a tutorial on "Drawing Buildings", go to:
Claudia's Art Therapy YouTube Channel

NOW IT'S YOUR TURN!

Find a building you would like to draw (you can use a picture or a nearby building to practice). Use the steps on the previous page to draw the building. Don't forget your shadows!

DRAWING A WALL OR LANDSCAPE

In order to draw in perspective, you must measure the objects. You may use a pencil to measure.

WHEN MEASURING OBJECTS:

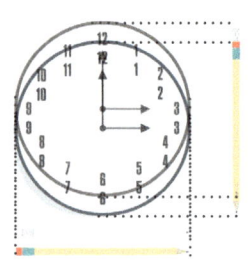

- Close one eye & hold your pencil up.

- Align top of pencil with the top of the object you are measuring.

- Place your thumb in line with the bottom side of the object you are measuring.

- The distance between the top of your pencil & your thumb will be the height* of the object on your paper.

   *when measuring width, do the same thing, but turn your pencil sideways.

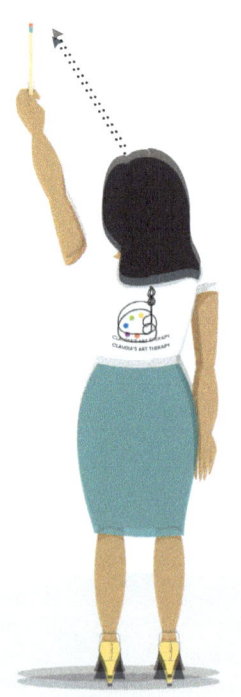

- When measuring something larger, you may use your hands.
- Remember to close one eye.
- With your left hand make this shape
- With your right hand make this shape
- The distance between your hands will be the size of the object on your paper.*

*This technique can be tricky. Please watch Claudia's tutorial for a demonstration.

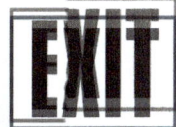
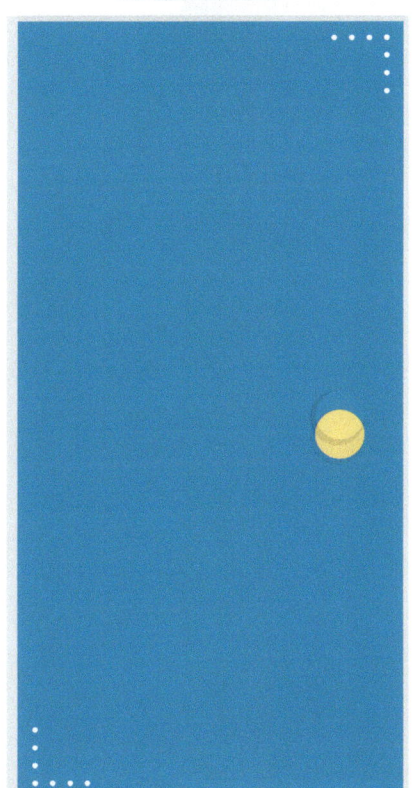
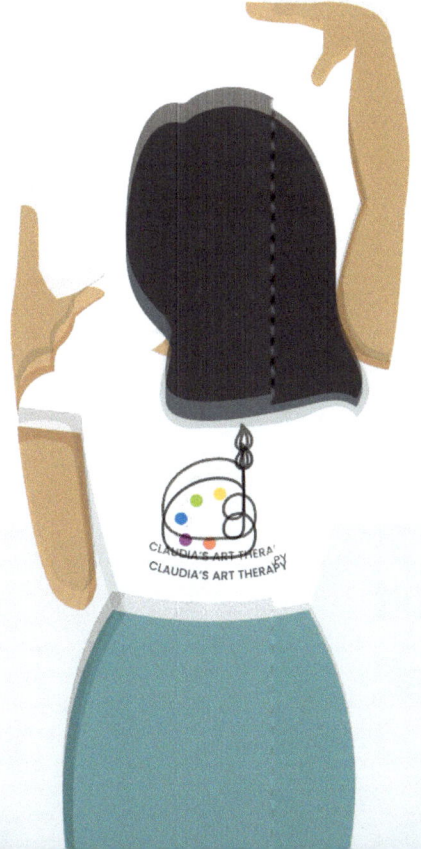

For a tutorial on "Drawing a Wall or Landscape", go to:
Claudia's Art Therapy YouTube Channel

ANIMALS & TEXTURES

Look for hidden shapes.
Draw mass before detail.
When adding hair, start from base/body.

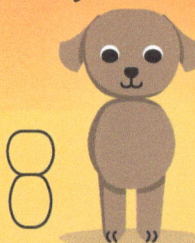

Rounded square

Rounded rectangles

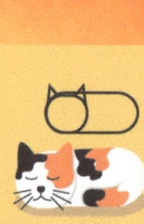

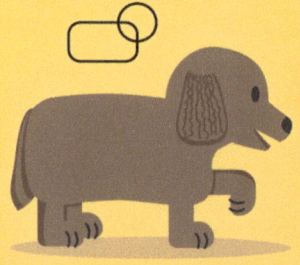

Rounded rectangle & circle

Legs (stockings)

Add tail

Oval body

Circle head

Triangle ears

Add tail

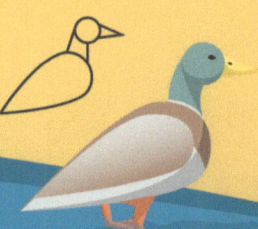

Teardrop

Rounded square

Circle

Triangle

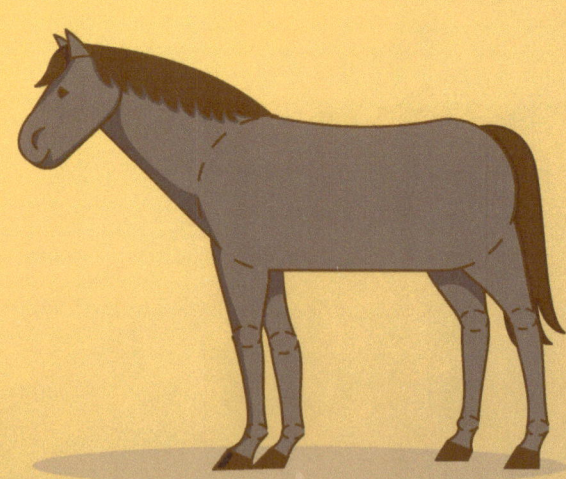

Ovalish body

Rectangle neck

Oval head

Four ovals (knees & ankles)

Connect legs

Remove guidelines

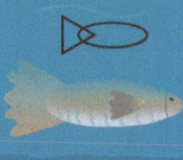

Oval & triangles

TEXTURES

You may use these textures to shade & add dimension to your sketch.

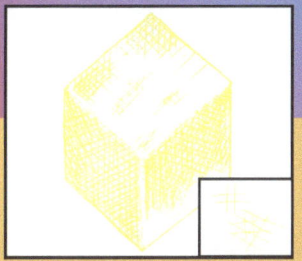

Cross hatching - use tic-tac-toe lines to texture your sketch.

Stippling - create a soft texture by dotting your sketch.

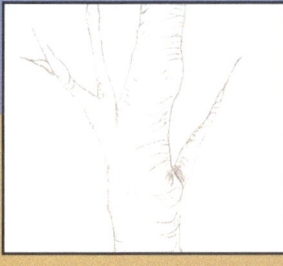

Bracelet shading - create this rough texture by drawing curved, uneven lines that mimic the curve of your subject.

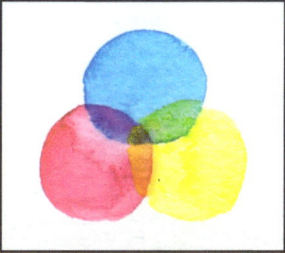

Glazing - layering paint over paint that has already dried.

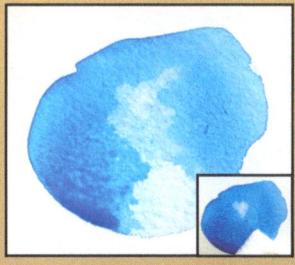

Blotting - to remove excess paint with a tissue or napkin.

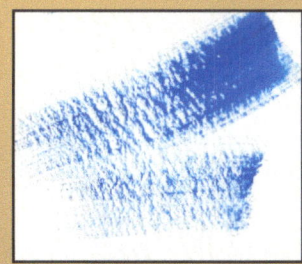

Dry brush - a technique in which a paint brush is very dry, but still has some paint.

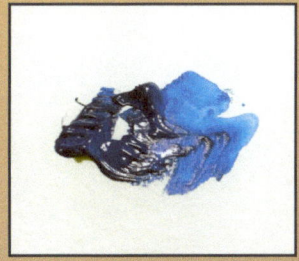

Impasto - a thick layer of paint that stands out from the surface.

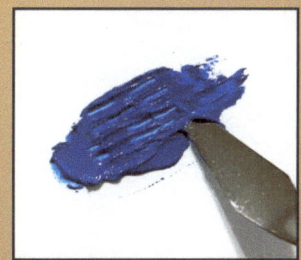

Sgraffito - "scratched" in Italian. You may use your fingernail or a palette knife to scratch paint.

For a tutorial on "Animals & Textures", go to:
Claudia's Art Therapy YouTube Channel

www.ingramcontent.com/pod-product-compliance
Lightning Source LLC
Chambersburg PA
CBHW051938210526
45473CB00006B/2295